I0453368

Let's vibe!

@zenfulnote

Share a picture or video of your book on
TikTok or Instagram for
20% OFF your next purchase!

DM @zenfulnote or email
keila@zenfulnote.com with your post link
to receive your special discount.

1. PRELUDE

2. ENERGY PSYCHOLOGY

2. POETRY SERIES

The
VIBRATIONAL
POETRY BOOK

Also by Keila Shaheen:

The Shadow Work Journal
The 369 Manifestation Journal
The Gratitude Journal

To the daring who look up at the stars and wish.
To the one near yet so far. This book is dedicated to you,
whose reading this. May these poems be a source of comfort, inspiration,
and enlightenment on your journey through life.
May they remind you that you are not alone
and that there is beauty to be found in
the world around us.

THE DREAMER
AND THE DREAMED

\-

prelude

The Dreamer and The Dreamed

Thousands of years ago, there was a woman named Sanap. She was born with a gift from a very young age. She was able to sense the spiritual forces of the world, feel the true intentions of people's hearts, and receive messages in her dreams. However, it had been years since she had dreamt. Sanap dismissed her gifts as something of the past. One day, she noticed that a bird's nest was being attacked by a raccoon, and she ran outside to protect it. Gently, Sanap relocated the nest to another tree and spotted the mother bird perched up against a branch. Her wings stretched wide open, revealing a bright orange eye on each side. The mother bird dropped a smooth pebble into Sanap's hands and retreated back to her nest.

That night, Sanap dreamed quite unexpectedly. In her dream, she was walking down a street in a foreign city, and suddenly her hand lifted upwards to point toward the sky. "Look up!" she heard a voice. "I'm here," it whispered. The sky was filled with patterns of lines intersecting in a geometric fashion. It shifted as Sanap's focus did. She could see patterns in the sky turn from flowers to 6-pointed stars, to kaleidoscope figures. Even though the lines did not move, with a slight shift in perception, Sanap saw different images. It was much like an illusion.

7

"Mother bird's eyes" she whispered as the pattern revealed those big eyes she'd noticed the day before from the bird's wings. Sanap realized that whatever shape she imagined; the sky reflected. Her arm dropped heavily, and so did her gaze. She was frozen in awe, and could not move her arms and legs. Sanap woke up sweating. Something happened inside of her that transformed her completely. She ran outside to look up at the sky, full of stars. "We are all made up of the same patterns", she said. "This nature, this world, this space, these people are all created by light and ruled by the systems of the light", she whispered. Sanap knew that there was harmony between the systems of our universe and humanity. And that the system that created us is merely a fractal branch of the system that created our universe.

This is what she discovered: Everything is God. God is in the rocks, the birds, the waves, the air, the hands, the people, the matter, and beyond. And she came to the conclusion that everything is a reflection of this light. Every thought and focus manipulates the screen of reality that we experience. And mother bird's eye wasn't there completely, but with the focus of her mind, that is what appeared. She knew that it is not what you look at, but what you see. Everything that you see is a reflection of the current state and intention of your mind.

Light is the essence of the world,
It paints the sky and flowers,

It dances on the water's trace,
And warms the earth's kind face,

But light is not just what we see,
It's also what we choose to be,

For our thoughts can transform,
The way that light bends and shapes,

So what we see is but a mirror,
Of our mind's love or fear,

So let us choose with our care and our thought,
The light that guides us as we're taught.

Emotional Vibration

Emotions are energy in motion. All energy vibrates at a certain frequency, and frequency holds information. "The Vibrational Poetry Book" is a collection of poems that seek to explore the depths of our emotional landscape, inspired by the transformative power of energy psychology.

In energy psychology, it is believed that emotions carry specific vibrational frequencies that correspond to different states of being. Just as different musical notes create distinct melodies, emotions vibrate at various frequencies, each carrying its own unique information. This concept suggests that our emotions are not random or chaotic but rather part of a coherent energetic pattern. By attuning to the vibrational frequencies evoked through the poems, you can learn to navigate your emotions with greater ease and grace. This poem book serves as a reminder that emotions are not obstacles to overcome but valuable sources of information.

Our emotions hold tremendous power, shaping not only our inner reality, but also influencing the way we perceive and interact with the world around us. When we experience emotions, our body responds by releasing various neurochemicals (like hormones and neurotransmitters) which can have a profound impact on our physical well-being. Our emotions serve as a lens through which we view our reality, often tinting our experiences and affecting the decisions we make. Through intentional practice and self-reflection, we can learn to consciously shift our emotional states towards higher vibrational frequencies. This process involves becoming aware of our emotional patterns and consciously choosing thoughts, beliefs, and actions that align with our desired state of being.

Our emotions, thoughts, and beliefs are not just psychological phenomena, but also deeply intertwined with the intricate network of energy systems that govern our bodies.

By coming face-to-face with our energies vibrational state of being, we create more room for empathy, understanding, and compassion. We can begin to consciously shift our emotional states upwards, fostering a greater sense of balance, resilience, and harmony within ourselves. As we journey through this process of emotional alchemy, we are not only promoting our own well-being, but also cultivating a deeper connection to the world around us and manifesting a more fulfilling and authentic life experience.

1. The Emotional Guidance Scale

The emotions we feel become the energy we emit.

Our energy attracts its likeness. When we're low on the emotional scale, we're emitting negative energy, which attracts people, situations, and experiences that match that vibration. This is why some days seem to go from "bad" to "worse". This is why you go from receiving a stressful text, to losing your keys, to having your car break down and so forth. But it is also the reason why on some days you receive a text from an old friend you were thinking of, are offered new exciting opportunities, and experience ongoing occurrences of bountiful bliss.

Within the emotional guidance scale, you'll discover 17 unique emotional states, each resonating with its distinct vibrational frequency. From the denser vibrations of fear and despair to the lighter, more expansive feelings of joy and love, the scale invites you to a trek through a beautiful path of emotional forestry. At times, you may find yourself submerged in the heavier emotions, weighed down by feelings of disconnection, powerlessness, or self-doubt. But fear not, for these emotions have their place in the grand scheme of things, offering valuable lessons and insights. It is important to honor and validate your feelings, providing yourself with the time and space necessary to process and *really* feel them. However, remaining in these emotional states for too long can cast a shadow over your well-being and impede your growth.

These higher states of emotion, rich with a sense of connection, empowerment, and positive self-perception, will not only enhance your own well-being but also attract uplifting experiences and opportunities into your life.

Patience, persistence, and a willingness to embrace the full spectrum of your emotions will be key to this book.

It is important to note that your life experience is constantly moving through ebbs and flows, and this guidance scale is not to be thought of as a hierarchical ladder in which you "achieve" higher levels of enlightenment. Every emotion holds more worth and weight than gold, and you must embrace each one with an open, receptive heart and mind.

On the following pages, we will explore 2 frameworks for viewing our range of emotions. For the sake of organization and this book's layout, we will explore vibrational poetry through a linear fashion from chapters 1- 17 reflecting the emotional frequencies 1- 17.

STRUCTURE 1: EMOTIONAL VIBRATION SCALE

Emotions are energy in motion. All energy vibrates at a certain frequency, and frequency holds information.

HIGH

ENLIGHTENMENT

PEACE

JOY

LOVE

REASON

ACCEPTANCE

WILLINGNESS

NEUTRALITY

COURAGE

PRIDE

ANGER

DESIRE

FEAR

GRIEF

APATHY

GUILT

SHAME

HIGH

Bliss
- Passion
- Freedom
- Love
- Appreciation
- Enlightenment

CENTER

Anger
- Hatred/rage
- Jealousy
- Worried, doubtful
- Irritation
- Pessimism

LOW

Sadness
- insecurity/guilt
- Unworthiness
- Fear/grief
- Powerlessness
- Victim
- Shame

HIGH

CENTER HIGH

CENTER LOW

LOW

When emotions make an imprint on the subconscious mind, it begins to attract experiences that bring more of those emotions into our realities.

STRUCTURE: EMOTIONAL CIRCLE

All emotions are universal and experienced by every being in no single order. All are sacred in their own contexts, and carry deep wisdom for us.

PEACE   GRIEF

JOY   SADNESS

LOVE   FEAR

REASON   ENLIGHTENMENT

DESIRE   ACCEPTANCE

WILLINGNESS   APATHY

NEUTRALITY

GUILT   COURAGE

PRIDE

ANGER   SHAME

Experience ebbs and flows of emotion fully rather than trying to climb up the illusional ladder of enlightenment.

How to use this book

This book serves as a beacon to guide you inwards in order to fully experience and synthesize your feelings rather than push them aside. Each chapter's ending will provide you with resources and guidance to experience a higher state of vibrational awareness.

To begin this path, you must:

1. *Consciously cultivate your thoughts. The poems aligned with your present emotional state will facilitate a deeper connection with your feelings. The affirmations and resources concluding each chapter will assist you in reevaluating your emotions and fostering elevated vibrational thoughts.*

2. *Be willing to recognize and experience your emotions.*

This book is not designed to be perused in a linear fashion. Recognizing the fluid nature of our emotional experiences and the non-linear path towards enlightenment, I advise that you use the guided meditation (*page 17*) to help identify your current emotional vibration each time you visit this poem book.

5-STEP MEDITATION
FOR EMOTIONAL AWARENESS

next ⟶

STEP 1:

FIND A COMFORTABLE POSITION.
SIT OR LIE DOWN IN A
COMFORTABLE POSITION WHERE
YOU WON'T BE DISTURBED FOR THE
NEXT FEW MINUTES.

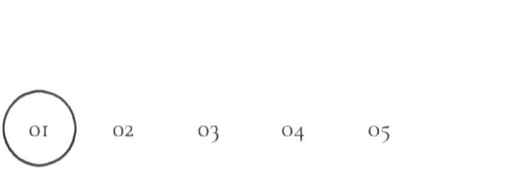

01   02   03   04   05

STEP 2:

INHALE DEEPLY THROUGH YOUR NOSE FOR 4 SECONDS. AS YOU INHALE, FEEL YOUR BELLY EXPAND AND YOUR CHEST RISE.

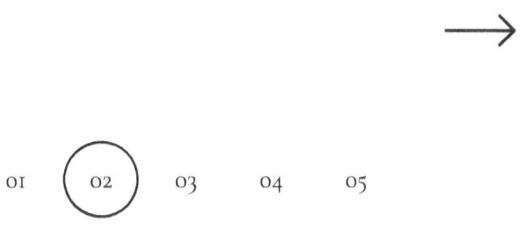

01　02　03　04　05

STEP 3:

SHIFT YOUR FOCUS TO YOUR BODY. NOTICE
SENSATIONS YOU ARE FEELING, LIKE THE AIR ON
YOUR SKIN, THE WEIGHT OF YOUR BODY ON
YOUR FEET.

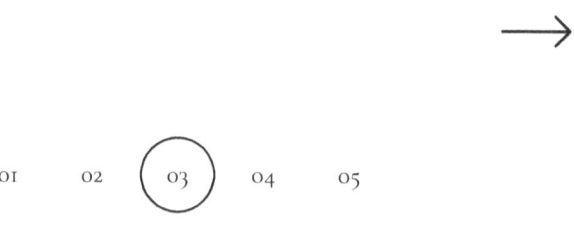

01   02   03   04   05

STEP 4:

BRING YOUR ATTENTION TO YOUR EMOTIONS.
NOTICE ANY FEELINGS OR SENSATIONS THAT
ARE PRESENT IN YOUR BODY, WITHOUT
JUDGING THEM OR TRYING TO CHANGE THEM.
SIMPLY ACKNOWLEDGE AND ALLOW THEM TO
BE THERE.

$\longrightarrow$

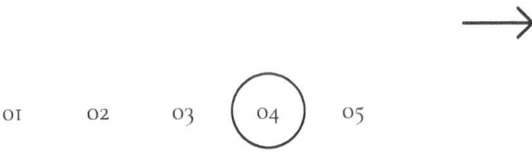

01   02   03   (04)   05

STEP 5:

TAKE A FEW MORE DEEP BREATHS, AND CONTINUE TO FOCUS ON YOUR SURROUNDINGS, YOUR BODY, AND YOUR EMOTIONS. AS YOU DO, YOU MAY FIND THAT YOU BECOME MORE AWARE OF YOUR EMOTIONAL STATE.

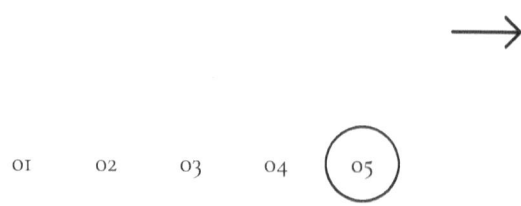

01   02   03   04   (05)

FIND YOUR FEELING.
FLIP TO THE CORRELATING CHAPTER.

Bliss
- Passion
- Freedom
- Love
- Appreciation
- Enlightenment

CENTER

Anger
- Hatred/rage
- Jealousy
- Worried, doubtful
- Irritation
- Pessimism

LOW

Sadness
- insecurity/guilt
- Unworthiness
- Fear/grief
- Powerlessness
- Victim
- Shame

1. *SHAME*

I stand before the mirror,
And see the person I've become,
A stranger to myself,
And everyone.

Shame will humble you, sit you down,
take you to the corner of the room,
face you up against the wall.

Shame will zero out the whole world around
you,
and punish you for,
being at all.

Perhaps, if we were all rudely alive,
we'd eat the bread of Mercy,
than starve in the void of shame.

Today I felt like a star dimming, and flickering, and spiraling out of control. Head pounding with frustration, throat shriveled and aching. Inflamed from shame.

In the morning, I woke up emotionally hungover.
But *feeling* was *healing.*
Crying was *cleansing.*
Today is welcoming.

I catch myself mid-cringe,
watching online portrayals,
and turn over the hand-held mirror,
of judgement,
only to reveal internalized shame.

To hide who you are,
because you do not believe you are
worthy,
is like refusing to eat,
because you think you are allergic to
food.

It is your birthright to live authentically,
to quench the hunger of your soul.

Trauma is when you fall into a hole, and get back out different.
Adapted to holes. You spend the rest of your life on high alert,
looking out for holes not to fall in. You'll forget to look at the insects.
You'll forget to look at the sky. You'll forget the way the world was
before that big black lie.

MOVE THROUGH SHAME

AFFIRMATIONS

I am loved- despite my shame.
My discomfort will not last forever.
It's just a feeling. I allow myself to let go.
I let go of guilt and shame. I love and approve of myself.
I am safe and sound. All is well.

REFLECTIVE QUESTIONS:

1. How does shame manifest in my life, and how does it affect my thoughts, emotions, and behaviors?
2. What triggers shame within me, and what are the underlying beliefs or expectations that contribute to these feelings?
3. In what ways does shame limit me from fully expressing myself and pursuing my goals and desires?

MORE OF THIS:

- Become aware. Accept your feelings.
- Go outside and spend time in nature
- Practice mindfulness.
- Recognize your inner critic.

2. *GUILT*

chapter 2

Love is like a thief.
Not a thief in the night,
but a thief in the day,
who knows what to give,
in order to take.

Guilt is a villainous tale. After a few days of it, I drift into the pages of an untold story, slipping among obstacles in a jagged woodland. The sky echoes my thoughts only, and when I speak, dense trails of wilderness hush my words mute. A few days of wrestling with vines leaves me worn, and I let go. Rest is needed. I reawaken, detached, and see trails of light paving me back to reality. I'm coming home.

Gentle reminders as you heal:

1. *You can start over at any time.*
2. *Create inner space through your breath.*
3. *It's okay when things don't go as planned.*
4. *You are allowed to protect your time and energy.*
5. *Rest. Rest. Rest.*

This is your reminder to not let your
disappointments make you lose hope.

Guilt says you're wrong,
Shame says you're not smart enough,

Guilt says you're weak,
Shame says you're not strong enough,

Guilt says you're too late,
Shame says you're not fast enough.

All mouths sing the same song,
In a different key.

What does love say?

Is it a sin to take the Sun? On this summer's day?

To bathe in its moist molasses,
let it glaze every corner of my body,
to the point of reflection.

They don't tell you to make love like this.
They wouldn't know that this is the closest
To the Sun you can get.

MOVE THROUGH GUILT

AFFIRMATIONS
• *I forgive myself for any mistakes and choose to learn from them.* • *I am doing my best, and that is enough.* • *I let go of guilt and move forward with love and wisdom.*

REFLECTIVE QUESTIONS:

1. What actions can I take to address the root cause of my guilt?
2. How can I practice self-forgiveness and move forward?
3. What values can guide me in making future decisions?

MORE OF THIS:

- Making amends or apologizing where necessary
- Identifying and challenging guilt-inducing thoughts
- Reflecting on personal values and aligning actions with them

3. APATHY

chapter 3

Dopamine hits everywhere,
we take them selfishly like candy,
and wonder why we feel so empty,
without it.

I think the world,
is ironic.
Like an ill doctor,
or a noisy bird watcher.

We hold the root,
to all of our problems,
and blame every other factor,
but ourselves.

I lost
My spark.

Some days I feel like the main character,
Some days I feel like an outcast.
But most days I'm in the audience,
Watching as they play their parts.

It's a beautiful, ironic, romantic, sad, climatic play.

Who else is in the audience?

I used to laugh at bare trees,
and call them naked,
now I shiver with them in the winter,
when my heart feels vacant.

I LAUGHED TODAY,
BUT THE SILENCE THAT ACCOMPANIED IT,
MOCKED ME.

THE QUIET RESIDUE,
WAS HEAVY.

IT HUNG FROM MY EARS LIKE A NUMB LIMB,
MY HEART IS DRY NOW,
A RAISIN IN THE SUN.

MOVE THROUGH APATHY

AFFIRMATIONS

- *I choose to re-engage with life, embracing curiosity, and passion.*
- *I have the power to cultivate motivation, excitement, and purpose.*
- *I am open to new experiences and possibilities that inspire my soul.*

REFLECTIVE QUESTIONS:

1. What underlying factors may be contributing to my feelings of apathy, and how can I address them constructively?
2. What activities, relationships, or aspects of life have brought me joy and passion in the past? How can I reconnect with those experiences and incorporate them into my present life to combat apathy?
3. How does apathy affect my sense of connection and empathy towards others?

MORE OF THIS:

- Connect with others. Engage in open and honest conversations, and share experiences.
- Setting small, achievable goals to reignite motivation and sense of accomplishment
- Exploring new hobbies, interests, or experiences that spark excitement.

4. GRIEF

chapter 4

All I see are mouths moving,
through the corner of my eyes,
and I respond, to my surprise.

How can I be there and here,
At the same time?

Healing is not suppressing your emotions when managing
your reactions. But rather to feel. To journey down each emotion.
To identify each memory associated with it. Tend to it.
Learn its origin. And as you gently massage the roots of your suffering,
you will find more space for understanding and compassion.

Within this space, is healing.

You'll find your greatest enemy,
in your darkest shadows,
and in befriending them,
you will be at peace with,
every part of you.

Part of me has departed,
With you.

What is grief, but love inverted, flipped inside out,
hung upside down.

A love that oozes not from the full heart,
but from the empty pain of absence.

Why does life have to be so brief? You know, we talk about the "chapters"' in life, starting new ones and ending old ones. But in the end, our stories dissolve from a novel to a letter. Then, a one-liner on a tombstone, when read, is resurrected in curious, momentary thought.

MOVE THROUGH GRIEF

AFFIRMATIONS

- *I honor my feelings of grief, allowing space for healing and growth.*
- *I am supported and loved as I navigate through grief.*
- *I cherish the memories and connections, knowing that love is never truly lost.*

REFLECTIVE QUESTIONS:

1. How can I validate and honor my feelings of grief while also remembering that healing takes time?
2. What support systems or resources can I access to help me navigate through this difficult period?
3. How can I cherish and honor memories of people or situations, while also allowing space for personal growth and healing?

MORE OF THIS:

- Practicing self-compassion, patience, and understanding as you move through grief
- Allowing space for emotional expression through journaling, art, or talking with people you love
- Honoring memories of people or situations through rituals or personal reflection

5.FEAR

chapter 5

Even a palace,
Can be a prison.

Even an angel,
Can be a villain.

Even the sunlight,
Can cast a shadow.

Even the fondest memories,
Can be faux.

Fear, an unmet guest,
Yet, through unknown, we are blessed,
Life's test, undressed.

Maybe the real reason you dread,
the things you know you need to do,
is because you are so afraid of losing yourself,
during the evolution,
because action leads to growth,
and growth requires shedding,
and shedding requires you,
to let go.

We built a fortress out of fears,
and relish in them silently,
like kings and queens.

How do we wake,
a dormant spirit,
when life is the dream,
we sleep right through it.
Our minds succumb,
like blindfolds to the sun,
and like mice, we run,
like mice, we run.

Fear is a pain,
Too lonely to know,
That Life
Is its counterpart.

MOVE THROUGH FEAR

REFLECTIVE QUESTIONS:

1. What are the underlying beliefs or past experiences that contribute to these fears? Can I trace their origins and understand how they have shaped my perception of myself and the world?
2. Are these fears rational or based on assumptions? Can I gather evidence or alternative perspectives that challenge these fears and offer a more balanced outlook?
3. What small steps can I take today to confront and challenge my fears? How can I gradually build my courage and resilience to face them head-on?

MORE OF THIS:

- Visualize success: Use visualization techniques to imagine yourself successfully overcoming the fear-inducing situation.
- Practice self-compassion: Be kind and compassionate towards yourself as you face your fears.
- Challenge your fears: Question the validity of your fears.

6.DESIRE

chapter 6

A dream,
quenches the drought of reality,
don't speak with parched lips,
let them soak in honey and sugar.
Speak with your heart and let yourself disobey your mind,
at least from time to time.

"Isn't it crazy how 3 choices you could make today could change your life?"

1. A move to a new city.
2. A call to a lost love.
3. A simple walk in the park.

"But we make the same choices every day."

The **knowing** of what to expect gives our minds stability.
But in the knowing, we distance ourselves from life itself.

What 3 choices will you make today?

How foolish was I,
to think,
I needed more,
to feel satisfied with life.

It is June.
Nothing is asked of me.
Like a kid's summer dream.
The candle's flame is still,
As am I.

Desires that stem from irritation are ego-aligned.
Desires that stem from peace are soul-aligned.

Sparks fly,
in my chest,
when all my doubts are laid to rest,
when all my dreams beat fiercely,
against the thin layer between thought and reality,
they hatch through the wall,
emerging, more beautifully than I ever imagined.

Eyes speak to eyes,
Iin glances as clear as daylight.
They flash each other,
in plain sight,
and mingle under the moonlight.

MOVE THROUGH DESIRE

AFFIRMATIONS

- *I embrace my desires, using them as a source of motivation and inspiration.*
- *I trust in the abundance of the universe, knowing that my desires can be fulfilled.*
- *I am open to the opportunities and experiences that align with my true desires.*

REFLECTIVE QUESTIONS:

1. How do my desires align with my core values, and how can I use them as a source of motivation and growth?
2. What specific steps can I take to manifest my desires into reality while maintaining balance and self-care?
3. How can I cultivate an abundance mindset, trusting that the universe will provide the opportunities and experiences necessary to fulfill my desires?

MORE OF THIS:

- Reflecting on your desires and motivations to ensure they come from a soul-aligned space
- Setting clear, achievable goals that align with your desires
- Developing a plan of action to manifest your desires into reality
- Practicing visualization techniques to create a mental image of your desired outcomes

7. ANGER

chapter 7

When my body emits a dark aura,
my face turns stone and words run dry.

I know something is wrong,
I know something's is off.

Before I let it consume,
I look for myself in the mirror,
I become an observer of my body:

> *"How do I feel?"*
> *"How do I move?"*
> *"Where is my breath?"*

Sometimes you must walk backwards with blindfolds and let
conscious awareness pull you back to the center of the spiral.

When anger furls inside your chest, through your arms,
and into your clenched fists   put your heart to rest.
Let your fingers sway. Resist.

Go against the tension of suffering.
Shake, jump, dance, hug yourself, kiss your shoulders, take
a bow; exhale in every possible way that you can.
The next breath with cleanse you.

Anger can be blue,
Vast and all-consuming like the sky.

Anger can be black,
An unimaginably deep absence of light.

Anger can be burgundy,
Bright, fierce, turned dull, like a scab.

May we use anger's pallet,
To add rich depth into our lives.

Sometimes anger is beautiful, transformative,
The anger of when you've had enough,
The anger that makes you set boundaries,
The anger that transforms passivity into change.

This anger signals that you are ready for more.

Anger is,
your inner child,
throwing a tantrum.
What needs are you screaming for,
that have not been met?

Once you drink the poison of rage,
It will first boil your blood.

Then, the poison will seep into your mind,
blurring the lens of thought with a thick
cloud of anger.

Next, it will take your body over.
You will act on impulse rather than
contemplation.
Your aura will darken, and you will not
recognize this version of you.

The antidote; a sip from the well of peace.
Yes, simple, yet far from reach. Minimize the
distance between yourself and peace with a
breath, a bare foot to the earth, and
reminders of love.

MOVE THROUGH ANGER

AFFIRMATIONS

- *I release anger and choose to respond with love and understanding.*
- *I am in control of my emotions and reactions.*
- *I transform anger into positive action and growth.*

REFLECTIVE QUESTIONS:

1. What is the underlying cause of my anger, and how can I address it constructively?
2. How can I express my emotions assertively without causing harm?
3. What positive actions can I take to transform my anger into growth?

MORE OF THIS:

- Practicing assertive communication
- Identifying triggers and developing healthy coping strategies
- Channeling anger into creative or physical outlets

8.PRIDE

chapter 8

We swirl our spoons inside the same jar of honey,
beating the batter of joy until there's nothing left
but a lick of laughter and a hollow bowl.

Pride says,
We are large,
And they are small,
But without the lens,
There's no size at all.

Pride gallivants,
Blindly,
With a joker's face,
And ends its dance,
In humility's disgrace.

More leads to
More leads to
More leads to
More leads to
More! Leads to
More!! Leads to
More!! More!! More!!
Leads to nothing.

Pride creates the illusion of a separate self.

When your pride overflows,
and spills onto everyone else's clothes,
accept the task to clean,
the mess of your scene.

Pride will ruin the most fruitful relationships.

Cast away your self righteousness. Ask why.
Make an effort to understand. Apologize.

Everybody wants love, but nobody wants to sacrifice.

MOVE THROUGH PRIDE

AFFIRMATIONS

- *I celebrate my accomplishments with humility and gratitude.*
- *I acknowledge my strengths and talents, while also recognizing the contributions of others.*
- *I strive for personal growth and self-improvement, knowing that there is always room to learn and grow.*

REFLECTIVE QUESTIONS:

1. How can I celebrate my accomplishments and strengths in a way that is balanced and inclusive of others?
2. What opportunities are available for me to give back, support others, or engage in acts of service?
3. How can I cultivate a healthy self-esteem that values personal growth, humility, and connection with others?

MORE OF THIS:

- Practicing gratitude for personal achievements and the achievements of others
- Sharing and celebrating accomplishments in a balanced manner
- Engaging in volunteering to give back

9. COURAGE

chapter 9

I look outside my window,
There is nothing to see,
Then I flip over my phone,
There is nothing to see.

Then I go back to my window,
Seeking harder than before,
Then I start to see the magic,
That I had missed once more.

You see, searching is the blindfold,
And seeing is the treasure.

I will remain in my dreams forever. I will keep reality nebulous and vague and leave room for imagination; creativity-inducing mind fog. I wander around this realm where ideas seem to multiply. There is no wrong or right, only fertile ground for expansion and creation.

Life is a myriad of a thousand miracles.
Notice each one of them. Including yourself.

There once was a little sad panda.
Had tears streaming from his eyes,
Had no bamboo for him to hide,
Felt naked in the sun,
Because he and the night were one.
One day, the sky asked him:
"Panda, why are you sad?"
He buried his head,
Said he had no one to smile with,
The sky gave a cry,
Water punched the ground,
Then grass began to grow,
Panda heard a sound,
Giggles in the air coming from all
around,
His mouth began to shiver,
As flowers burst into laughter,
Panda smiled at last!
And lived happily ever after.

Music is medicine,
Community is medicine,
Nature is medicine,
Laughter is medicine,
Hugs are medicine,
Art is medicine,
Movement in medicine,
Stillness is medicine.

You are medicine. Or
poison.
Decide for yourself.

Little tree,
In the mound,
What makes you so?
What makes you ground?
Your roots like hands,
Grip earth's core,
Holding tight
forevermore.

MOVE THROUGH COURAGE

AFFIRMATIONS

- *I boldly step outside my comfort zone and embrace new experiences.*
- *I am brave and confident in expressing my true self.*
- *I face uncertainty with courage and adaptability.*
- *I release all doubts and trust in my inner wisdom.*

REFLECTIVE QUESTIONS:

1. What specific fears or challenges can I face with courage and determination, and what steps can I take to do so?
2. How can I embrace new experiences and opportunities for growth, even when they feel uncomfortable or challenging?
3. What sources of inspiration can I draw upon to cultivate courage and resilience in my daily life?

MORE OF THIS:

- Identifying areas of personal growth or challenges and taking small steps to face them
- Embracing new experiences, opportunities, and learning to expand your comfort zone

10. NEUTRALITY

chapter 10

The space between
"not anymore"

and

"not yet"
Is an ego death. Honor it.

I would love to be home,
but I'm not entirely sure,
where that is.

Welcome to the vibrational equilibrium,
the purgatory of presence,
a separation of thought and movement.
Just a human being,
Being. Nothing more. Nothing less.

Who needs companionship,
When you could just sit on your porch and listen.

Don't be fooled by the radio, the TV, or the magazines,
they'll show you photographs,
of how your life should be.
But they're just someone else's fantasy.
So if you think your life is complete confusion,
because you never win the game-
just remember life's a Grand illusion,
and deep inside, we're all the same.

Your subconscious,
is a fly on the wall.
Be careful,
with the words, the thoughts,
the intentions and the actions,
in the room of your mind,
because the walls listen,
they'll continue building,
or fall a part.

MOVE THROUGH NEUTRALITY

REFLECTIVE QUESTIONS:

1. How can I cultivate a sense of neutrality and nonattachment in my daily life, allowing myself to observe more?
2. What specific practices or habits can I develop to enhance my ability to remain grounded, centered, and balanced in the face of life's fluctuations?
3. How can I maintain a sense of inner peace and harmony, even during challenging or emotionally charged situations?

MORE OF THIS:

- Practicing mindfulness meditations to enhance awareness and presence in the moment
- Engaging in grounding activities (yoga, spending time in nature) to connect with inner peace and equilibrium

11. WILLINGNESS

chapter 11

Deep within each one of us is pure brilliance, a force of light
and potential that can never be extinguished. Though it may be
petrified beneath layers of doubt or fear, it waits patiently to be
unleashed upon the world.

So ask yourself, *"When will I unleash my brilliance?"*

In this ripe moment, imagine what boundless possibility.
When all labels, roles, and identities are stripped away,
Who remains at the core of your being?

What habits are you?

Without human connection,
we are merely loose strings,
hanging for dear life,
waiting for a knot, a tie,
a meaning to our strife.
It's okay to get tangled,
life's too messy to be handled.
Just hang on tight,
because the tension,
is what makes us alive.

Beauty is as malleable as imagination.
They both only go as far as you'll recognize them.

What is stopping you?
What is pushing you?
The reason that wins will determine your soul's purpose.

You'll know when you're on the right path,
When you are unfazed by the things that once triggered you.

MOVE THROUGH WILLINGNESS

AFFIRMATIONS

- *I am open and receptive to new opportunities, experiences, and growth.*
- *I embrace change and the unknown with curiosity, courage, and adaptability.*
- *I am willing to learn, evolve, and become the best version of myself.*

REFLECTIVE QUESTIONS:

1. What does willingness mean to me? How would I describe the feeling or energy associated with being open and willing?
2. How can I inspire and encourage willingness in others? How can I create an environment that fosters openness, collaboration, and growth?

MORE OF THIS:

- Practice empathy and compassion
- Foster a growth mindset: Embrace a growth mindset that sees challenges and setbacks as opportunities for learning and growth
- Embrace curiosity

12. *ACCEPTANCE*

chapter 12

The number 11 followed me like an angel from heaven.

It was printed on the ticket home,
It was the day I wrote my first poem.

The number 11 played with my mind,
It popped up everywhere at the same exact time.

It was the time the plane took off,
It was what the candy at the store had cost.

It was the time the plane landed,
It was the chapter my life started.

The number 11,
Became a wild obsession.

It became the number "smile",
Because its presence was like a child's.

I found myself a friend,
One that feeds my imagination.

11 found me;
It's presence is concrete.

Pink dragon flies on my bare body.
Green moss pressing back onto my palms.
Holy water feeds these springs.
Gentle, messy, vibrant, browns, yellows,
Insects: deeply buzzing cellos.
Dare I make one move or one sound,
That disrupts this holy moment.

Snail shells, life's tale gently spun,
encased within their prints,
each whorl, a chapter in nature's grand design,
a testament to existence, truly divine.

In life,
There is no definition,
Or destination,
No day is the same,
No place is the end,
It's like building a mountain,
With a pile of sand.
Death is not anything at all,
Once energy exists, it is never destroyed,
Life is a full circle, but not a void,
In endless continuity, our lives begin,
Again, and
Again, and
Again...

Each day,
I play dress-up,
with my mind,
in songs.

They have colors and embellishments,
allowing me to curate,
the perfect fit of feeling,
for my human being.

It was a hushed morning,
5am felt like a secret.
The horizon,
beautiful and bruised,
gave birth to the sun,
and morning dew dissipated,
along with the residue of yesterday.
The sun is shining,
Today.

MOVE THROUGH ACCEPTANCE

AFFIRMATIONS

- *I embrace acceptance, welcoming all aspects of myself and my life without judgment.*
- *I find peace in understanding that life's events unfold as they are meant to be.*
- *I celebrate the beauty of diversity and the unique qualities within myself and others.*

REFLECTIVE QUESTIONS:

1. How can I cultivate a greater sense of acceptance toward myself, my life, and others, without judgment or resistance?
2. How can I extend acceptance to others? How can I create a space of non-judgment, understanding, and acceptance?

MORE OF THIS:

- Release control: Recognize and let go of the need to control outcomes or other people
- Challenge judgments and assumptions: Become aware of your judgments and assumptions about yourself and others.
- Self reflect: reflect on your thoughts, emotions, and reactions to situations.

13.REASON

chapter 13

"What are we?"
On the surface, our egos. Beneath the surface,
everything and nothing.

"What is our ego?"
It is all that we think we are. When we subtract the ego, we
subtract all that we know, and become all that is.

People interact in colors,
Many of us match, many don't,
Some of us transform our colors,
According to the surrounding tones,
Some of us cannot,
Most of us try,
But in the end,
Our colors either,
Mix or Match.

What meaning are you making,
out of every situation?

When you move at the speed of creation,
you start to become,
the creator (*and the creation*).

There are 3 voices that make up your human:
1. The mind
2. The mind-watcher (conscious awareness)
3. The subconscious (unconscious awareness)

The truth is lost at number 1.
The truth is revealed at number 2.
The truth is absorbed at number 3.

Without judgement, question yourself and your values-
"Why am I doing this?"
"Why does this bring me joy/sadness?"
"What are my roles?"

! The ego hates when you question every value you hold, and
when
you identify the roles you are playing.

Your mind is a jury's court. Sometimes the mind judges against you, against your truth, your purpose. In those times, you must be willing to have the strength to negotiate with your mind. Flip the script. Seek enough evidence to claim justice.

Your mind won't go against you when you give it enough reason to work with you.

MOVE THROUGH REASON

AFFIRMATIONS

- *I value the power of reason, using logic and critical thinking to navigate life's challenges and opportunities.*
- *I embrace clarity of mind, seeking to understand and learn from my experiences and emotions.*
- *I cultivate discernment and wisdom, making informed decisions that align with my values and goals.*

REFLECTIVE QUESTIONS:

1. How can I cultivate a greater sense of reason and critical thinking in my daily life, using these skills to navigate challenges and opportunities?
2. What specific practices or habits can I develop to enhance my ability to approach emotions and experiences with clarity and discernment?

MORE OF THIS:

- Reading, learning, and having stimulating conversations
- Practicing critical thinking and problem-solving skills to address challenges and opportunities

14.LOVE

chapter 14

Your love was like the rain,
After a drought.

Your love was like the sea,
After the pool.

Your love was like the sand,
After the gravel.

Your love was like a bed,
After a long travel.

I want. To strum your fingers. Like a kalimba. Like a game of thumb war. Knowing I will not win, but knowing I have won the grandeur game of life's pursuit to love. So I will pretend to wrestle your thumbs. With all my might. Just because it brings me. A bit closer. To you.

I wish to walk slowly,
to feel each step so deeply,
that walking turns into floating.

I wish for my bare feet,
to kiss the ground,
and drink its nectar of minerals through my skin.

I wish to follow nature's sequence,
to shed, wilt, grow, and prosper with it.
The closer I am to nature,
the deeper my understanding of self is.

You and me,
they and we,
are more connected,
then it may seem.
You see:
Love is everyone's dominant gene,
Love is in everyone's family tree,
Love is the breath of humanity,
Love is the stillness beyond the world's entropy.

Pour into what fills you up.

Your smile surpasses every word's attempt,
at making sense.
There is no expression,
For that smile,
but itself.
I'm left speechless,
breathless,
wordless,
under the spell,
of that bright white,
crescent sight,
your face,
is my sky,
and that smile,
lights up my life

MOVE THROUGH LOVE

AFFIRMATIONS

- *I am a beacon of love, radiating kindness and compassion to myself and others.*
- *I attract and nurture loving relationships, recognizing the interconnectedness of all beings.*
- *I celebrate the healing power of love, embracing its transformative and unifying force.*

REFLECTIVE QUESTIONS:

1. How can I cultivate a greater sense of love and compassion for myself and others in my daily life?
2. What specific practices or habits can I develop to nurture loving relationships, connection, and empathy within my community?
3. How can I embody love as a guiding force in my actions and decisions?

MORE OF THIS:

- Practicing loving-kindness meditations to cultivate compassion and empathy
- Engaging in acts of kindness and service
- Embracing self-love and learning how those around you best receive love

15. JOY

Silliness is
essential
to a happy life.

The world is filled with dots to connect,
Once the image is created, you realize it was you all along.
You held the pen. You moved the lines.
You are the creator. And the creation.

Grass excites me,
long, tall, plush,
from afar, a sea of green.

Wind blows and the grass ripples to the right,
stretching long like a yoga sequence,
taught by the wind,

I will learn to move with flow like grass.

Magic waves, I see you! Glistening at the pace of a static TV screen.
But instead of white dots, you shed sparkles onto the water.
Alive, you are!
And I with you. My sweat gleams against the sun, too.
All living things shine somehow.
Isn't that lovely?

We welcome joy,
such as an open mouth,
invites the first drop of rain,
in the summer.

And as the first drop,
descends,
grass begins,
it's ecstatic dance.

People emerge,
from their homes,
with blooming eyes,
they forage their laughter,
and hug each other.
Oh, joy! Endless joy.

How fast is our life?
Good question!
But I'd much rather know
Not how fast,
But how slow,
If I take a deep breath,
and create inner-depth,
Is it life that I'm in?
Where does it begin?

MOVE THROUGH JOY

AFFIRMATIONS

- *I embrace joy, celebrating the beauty and wonder of life in all its forms.*
- *I attract positive experiences and opportunities, cultivating a mindset of gratitude and happiness.*
- *I share my joy with others, spreading light and uplifting those around me.*

REFLECTIVE QUESTIONS:

1. How can I cultivate a greater sense of joy and happiness in my daily life, focusing on the beauty and wonder of the present moment?
2. What specific practices or habits can I develop to nurture a mindset of gratitude, positivity, and joy within my life and interactions with others?
3. How can I share my joy with those around me?

MORE OF THIS:

- Practicing gratitude, focusing on the abundance and blessings in your life
- Engaging in activities that bring joy, laughter, and playfulness
- Surrounding yourself with positive people and environments that inspire happiness and joy

16. PEACE

chapter 16

To live,
>On a see-saw,
Weighing both sides,
>With heavy,
Or light minds,
>A laugh,
A burden,
>A lighter love,

Peace is found in the equilibrium. When you
leave every light or heavy thought aside and seep
into your own body.

Non-traditional habits to cultivate stillness and appreciation:

1. At least once a week, initiate an impromptu journey by car to a public area. Go outside and start walking, be directed not by destination, but by curiosity. Witness how the symphony of the world conducts itself around you.

2. At any point in the day, when the urge to "do" spirals into a mental mountain, find a chair and sit on it. Starve yourself of movement and mental stimulation, watch yourself slowly melt into the clarity of Now.

3. Place your palms together, rub them up and down firmly, open your hands up like a book and, with your eyes, trace the intricate lines and valleys etched into your being, follow the curves as they rise and fall, imbuing your senses with a newfound appreciation.

It is not about forcing your way through. Softness opens doors that force cannot, like a seed that grows from stone, breaking through even the hardest of surfaces.

Ingredients of joy:

Someone you love,
The brush of a breeze,
A mouth full of dough,

A song made to move you,
A sunset in your purview,
A stroke of luck.

A glass full of water,
The patter of rain,
A laughter that chokes you.

An easy morning,
Mysterious caves,
Nostalgic games.

There's an orchestra in the background of my life,
Making every moment - no matter how silly or sad,
Seem like the climax.

Your stream of thought runs all day.
But deep peace is found whenever a gap occurs in the stream of
thought.
A subtle but intense joy fills the pause. The blankness.
The richness of being Here and Now.

Build a dam in your stream of thought.
Once you have learned to control and hold back your thoughts,
peace will flourish.

MOVE THROUGH PEACE

AFFIRMATIONS

- *I cultivate inner peace, harmonizing my thoughts, emotions, and actions with love and acceptance.*
- *I seek balance and tranquility in all aspects of my life, grounding myself in the present moment.*
- *I create a peaceful environment, fostering harmony and understanding within my relationships and community.*

REFLECTIVE QUESTIONS:

1. How can I cultivate a greater sense of peace and tranquility within my daily life?
2. What specific practices or habits can I develop to nurture a peaceful environment?
3. How can I maintain a balanced and centered state of being, grounding myself in the present moment and prioritizing self-care?

MORE OF THIS:

- Engaging in grounding activities, such as yoga, spending time in nature, or deep breathing exercises
- Pursuing conflict resolution and open communication to foster harmony and understanding within relationships and those around you

17. ENLIGHTENMENT

chapter 17

The perimeters of society
do not   exist
in that
of   nature.

Every thought surpasses itself,
reaching closer to understanding,
one realization leads to another,
a fractal of thoughts racing through and
out
of my mind.

To be enlightened is not to be above all else,
it is to be at every level of depth, to know
every soul with compassion and
understanding, while holding on to the truth
of love.

If you live in your desires, you are not present.
The breath has no past,
The breath has no future,
To be truly present,
Is to let go of your desires completely,
Because desire defines time,
Without desire, the watch has no arms.
Without desire, we hold eternal peace.

How to Breath: A Guide

1. *Awareness*

Your eye is a tool for grappling awareness. We live and roam mostly in our minds; use your eyes to step the legs of awareness into the physical world. Notice the corners of the room, the crown molding, how all the objects are square or round.

1. *Making room*

Now that you've stepped fully into existence, make space to sit or lay down. Clear the bed or the chair. Take a seat and get comfortable. Once you've found a room, and a seat, be still. Stay still until you can feel and hear your heart beating. This is vital. (pun intended)

1. *The inhalation*

Your first inhalation will not be your best. You'll have to face that. And it is okay because this is not a performance or a test. We are simply stepping on the breaks of unconscious automation by taking a controlled, thorough, cleansing breath. Breath again, and again. Sipping in as much air as your body can contain.

On your next breath, count your heartbeats as you inhale.

1. *The exhalation*

Did you forget about the exhalation? Ah, that is often the case. Let your exhale sound like something. Whatever sound comes out is right. Then, make sure your exhale is takes more heartbeats than your inhale. Continue inhaling and exhaling, with a beating heart as the guide.

Creation is a beautiful thing,
when you let God flow through you,
and come out the other side,
then step back and admire in awe.

Everyone is a vessel of God;
a channel for the divine.

Let's vibe!

@zenfulnote

Share a picture or video of your book on
TikTok or Instagram for
20% OFF your next purchase!

DM @zenfulnote or email
keila@zenfulnote.com with your post link
to receive your special discount.